The Gift of Christmas

Christmas

A 25-Day Devotional For Christmas

D1518746

Bradley W. Maston

DECEMBER 1ST

Genesis 3:14-15

"So the LORD God said to the serpent:
"Because you have done this,
You are cursed more than all cattle,
And more than every beast of the field;
On your belly you shall go,
And you shall eat dust
All the days of your life.
And I will put enmity between you and the woman,
And between your seed and her Seed;
He shall bruise your head and you shall bruise His heel."

Devotion

The story of Christmas starts at the very beginning of the Bible. It starts with the bad news. In order to fully appreciate the miracle that happened when Jesus Christ came to earth we must understand the gravity of the situation. God created a perfect world for humanity. He created Adam and Eve in His image. He created them to be finite versions of Himself and gave them stewardship over His good creation - the planet earth. He placed them in the garden and gave them a mission: "Then God blessed them, and God said to them, "Be fruitful and multiply; fill the earth and subdue it; have dominion over the fish of the sea, over the birds of the air, and over every living thing that moves on the earth." (Genesis 1:28).

He also gave them a single prohibition: "And the LORD God commanded the man, saying, "Of every tree of the garden you may freely eat; but of the tree of the knowledge of good and evil you shall not eat, for in the day that you eat of it you shall surely die." (Genesis 2:16-17). We know the rest of the story. Eve was deceived by the Serpent and ate the forbidden fruit. Adam disobeyed and did likewise and that is where everything went wrong. They did not physically die immediately - but they spiritually died at that very moment. They were separated from God at that point - the relationship was broken. There was nothing man could do to repair it.

When God laid out the resultant curse he also laid out mankind's only hope for salvation from sin. A hope that could only be provided by God Himself. He would provide the Savior through the line of man. The phrase "her seed" in Genesis 3:15 is a curious expression. This is the first hint that the Bible gives of the virgin birth of Jesus Christ. Seed is used in scripture for the male portion of the reproductive equation. Yet, the coming hope that would destroy the works of the Serpent (Satan) would be the seed of the woman and not of the man. Here at the very beginning of the story we see the hopeless position of man, and the hope that is given through Christ alone. Had He not been fully human he could not have identified with us to be our Savior. Had He not been fully God He could not have paid for all of the sins of the world. Were He not both man and God he would not be qualified to be our Savior and satisfy God's righteous wrath against sin.

This is what Christmas is about. Christmas is about God's great rescue plan being set into action right before our very eyes.

DECEMBER 2ND

Genesis 12:1-3

"Now the LORD had said to Abram:
"Get out of your country,
From your family,
And from your father's house,
To a land that I will show you.
I will make you a great nation;
I will bless you
And make your name great;
And you shall be a blessing.
I will bless those who bless you,
And I will curse him who curses you;
And in you all the families of the earth shall
be blessed."

Devotion

What does Abraham have to do with Christmas? Quite a bit! When God began His great rescue mission He told us that it would come through the lineage of mankind that He would provide the Savior. God is about to provide more information about the "seed" promise that He made in Genesis 3:15. God selected a family and made them the nation through which He would bring the Savior. God promised three things to Abraham: Land, Seed, and Blessing. The Land in question is the Land of Canaan - the literal physical land that the majority of the story of the Bible takes place. The Seed Promise was a promise that a great nation would come forth from Abraham. The Savior - the Promised seed of Genesis 3:15 would come through His line.

The covenant promise wouldn't go to all of Abraham's descendants, however. He chose Isaac over Ishmael or any of the other children of Abraham with His second wife Keturah. Of the two sons of Isaac, Jacob, the younger son, was chosen to carry the covenant promise forward. Esau was overlooked. Finally, the 12 tribes of Israel come forth to grow into the covenant community of the Nation of Israel - the Chosen Nation that would bring forth the Messiah.

All of these promises will ultimately be fulfilled in the Messianic Reign of Jesus Christ. God used the Nation of Israel, even in their disobedience, to bring blessing to all of the nations of the world. Jesus Christ is a descendant of Abraham. He is qualified to be the Savior. Through His work upon the cross salvation is available to anyone who trusts in His death, burial, and resurrection for our sin. (1 Corinthians 15:1-5).

DECEMBER 3RD

Genesis 49:8-12

"Judah, you are he whom your brothers shall praise;
Your hand shall be on the neck of your enemies;
Your father's children shall bow down before you.

Judah is a lion's whelp;
From the prey, my son,
you have gone up.
He bows down,
he lies down as a lion,
who shall rouse him?

The scepter shall not depart from Judah,
nor a lawgiver from between his feet.
Until Shiloh comes;
And to Him shall be the obedience of the people.
Binding his donkey to the vine,
And his donkey's cold to the choice vine,
He washed his garments in wine,

And his clothes in blood of grapes.
His eyes are darker than wine,
and his teeth whiter than milk."

Devotion

As the story of God's great rescue plan continued, the covenant promise was given to all of the children of Jacob. Each of Jacob's 12 sons would become the patriarch of a tribe of the Nation of Israel, and Joseph was given a double portion. This means that the counting of the tribes sometimes changes, but we find that no matter which way it is perceived the phrase "12 Tribes of Israel" always works as a collective title for the Nation which God selected.

At the end of Jacob's life he pronounced a prophetic blessing upon each of his sons that gives them key information about their descendants' role in God's plan. All of these prophetic messages are significant, but the promise to Judah is the one that makes the biggest impact on our celebration of Christmas. As the Lord reveals more and more about the coming Messiah it is clear that He will be a great ruling king of Israel. Thus it is important to know what tribe has the right of rulership in God's plan for Israel. God selected the tribe of Judah for this role.

The imagery of a lion, long known as the "king of beasts", is a sign of the authority of the tribe of Judah. Verse 10 makes this promise clearer still. The Scepter (the special stick that kings would use as a symbol of their reign) would not depart from Judah. The rulers of Israel were meant to come from the Tribe of Judah. Next it is revealed that the lawgiver would come from Judah's line. This is very interesting as Moses, who is of the tribe of Levi, was the one who gave Israel the Law (and wrote this very

11

account). How can this be? One could work around the problem by saying that the King is always a law-giver, even if "giving" means enforcing God's law. However, this is a Messianic statement. Moses delivered the Law - but it was given to them by the second person of the Trinity - the Son of God. This is a subtle illusion that the Messiah is Who is actually in view.

The third line of Genesis 49:10 reads (in the NKJV): "Until Shiloh comes." This is a curious phrase indeed. The word "Shiloh" doesn't appear again in the Bible until later (Joshua 18:1, 10; 22:12; Judges 18:31; 1 Samuel 3:21; and Psalm 78:60, et. al) and it is a place, not a person. However, Hebrew scholars give us an understanding of this word. The word "Shiloh" literally translates as "he to whom it belongs." The context makes it obvious! The rulers from the tribe of Judah would be, in a sense, place-holders until the True King - the actual Owner of that position would arrive...through the line of Judah. And He would be the one to Whom all the people gave obedience.

This prophetic statement awaits future fulfillment in the Messianic Kingdom, but it also informs our Christmas celebrations. Jesus Christ had to be born of the seed-line of Abraham, through Isaac, and through Jacob. The Messiah must also come through the line and tribe of Judah. We learn that he will be a king who will command the obedience of Israel and the World. Only Jesus fulfilled all of the requirements. The Savior came through the right lineage. We can know Him today by trusting in His perfect sacrifice for Sin at the Cross. In the Christmas season, we remember His first coming and celebrate it in anticipation of His second coming.

DECEMBER 4TH

Numbers 24:17

"I see Him,
     but not now;
I behold Him,
     but not near;

A Star shall come out of Jacob;
A Scepter shall rise out of Israel,
And Batter the brow of Moab,
and destroy all the sons of tumult."

Devotion

     Balaam is an interesting Bible character. He is a gentile and a genuine prophet. This shows that, though God's plan for salvation was through Israel, He never abandoned the gentile peoples of the earth. Balaam was by no means a perfect prophet. He knew that God had chosen Israel. He also knew that he could not pronounce any curse or blessing unless the Lord revealed it to Him. Initially, he stood strong on his convictions, but when the king of Moab, Balak, offered him enough money he agreed to come and entertain Balak's request to curse Israel. Numbers 22 records the story of how God miraculously gave Balaam's donkey the power of speech for a moment in order to save Balaam's life.

     As it turns out, Balaam was not able to curse the nation of Israel, though he tried at least four times. Nevertheless, the words that Balaam did give by means of special revelation were clear. God had chosen Israel, and nothing was going to cause God to give them up. In the context of one of Balaam's prophecies a special verse, Numbers 24:17, is placed. In this prophecy, Balaam sees a person, yet he is distant from where they are standing in time and space. This statement of distance shows that from the moment of this prophecy the figure being foretold was not coming soon from the perspective of Balaam. But He WAS coming!

     The picture of this coming figure as "a star" has great significance as to the Messiah's heavenly and eternal nature. The fact that he would come forth from Jacob shows the humanity of his lineage, and that He is called a star shows His divine nature. Moreover, it was likely this very promise that caused the Magi (the wise men from the east) to expect Christ's birth and travel to greet him as recorded in Matthew 2. How could they have known of this great prophecy? Quite easily, as it turns out.

Between 606 BC and 597 BC, the nation of Israel was relocated to Babylon in the east. Daniel was among the first groups of people to be deported along with his friends Shadrach, Meshach, and Abednego. Daniel rose to the highest levels of governmental authority as one of the king's wise men and served several administrations for both the Babylonian Empire as well as the Medo-Persian Empire. When the time came for Israel to be returned to the land the great majority of Jewish people stayed put in places like Babylon, Susa, and throughout the Empire and continued in important positions. This is illustrated in the book of Esther. Thus, they would have taken their Scriptures (the Torah and the former prophets) as well as kept the prophecies given to Daniel. The prophecies of Daniel gave them all the information that they needed. The Statue Prophecy given to King Nebuchadnezzar in a dream (Daniel 2), the Vision of the Beasts given to Daniel (Daniel 7), and the prophecy of the 70 weeks of years would have given them the timing of when they should be looking up for this unique astrological phenomenon that would lead them to see Him who was born King of Israel.

The Scepter that rises out of Israel is connected to the promise given to Judah in Genesis 49. This coming One would be a great ruler who would have complete dominance over all of His enemies. The Star Promise is yet more evidence that Jesus Christ came at exactly the right time, and even the heavens themselves declared His miraculous entry into our physical world. In the past, this prophecy led wise men to Him. So it does to this day.

DECEMBER 5TH

1 Chronicles 17:11-15

[11]"And it shall be, when your days are fulfilled,
when you must go to be with your fathers,
that I will set up your seed after you,
who will be of your sons;
and I will establish his kingdom.

[12]"He shall build Me a house,
and I will establish his throne forever.
[13]"I will be his Father, and he shall be My son;
and I will not take My mercy away from him,

as I took it from him who was before you.

[14]"And I will establish him in My house
and in My kingdom forever;
and his throne shall be established
forever."
[15] According to all these words and
according to all this vision, so Nathan
spoke to David.

Devotion

The Christmas story is about the arrival of the promised Messiah. Information was given so that the Nation of Israel could recognize Him when He came to them. Tragically, many missed His first coming, though they had the prophecies needed to recognize Him. They failed to own Him as their promised Redeemer. This led to the current church age when everyone has the opportunity to be saved by trusting in the Gospel of Jesus Christ. The promises of God are still clear in Scripture so that we might see clearly that this Child fulfills everything that God foretold about His first coming. That He, alone, is qualified to be Our Savior.

Another major qualification for the Messiah is given in what theologians call "The Davidic Covenant." This is another unconditional promise that God made revealing His plan to send Jesus to the earth. In the context of this passage David wanted to build a temple to worship God. Up to this point all of Israel's religious service was offered at the Tabernacle - a movable tent that housed the Ark of the Covenant, the Showbread, the Altar of Incense, the Golden Lampstand. Outside were the Laver for washing, and the Golden Altar for burnt offerings. David was told that he had been a man of war, and thus was disqualified to build God's house. His son, Solomon, would be given that honor. But in response God tells David that He (God) will build David's house.

The promises that are made to David are unconditional and first were applied to Solomon, but extend past Solomon to an Heir who would truly be the Son of God in a very unique way (speaking to the deity of Christ) and that His kingdom would be eternal and unending. From this important passage we learn that Jesus was, indeed, the ultimate fulfillment of that promise. The new information, given in this passage, is that the Messiah would be a descendant of David - in that Royal Line. We also see more clarity surrounding the Messianic Reign: once inaugurated, it would last forever.

This is a wonderful thing that we celebrate each Christmas. That Jesus is a descendant of David. He fulfills every requirement, and we look forward to His glorious reign upon the earth!

DECEMBER 6ᵀᴴ

Isaiah 7:10-14

10 Moreover the LORD spoke again to Ahaz, saying, 11 "Ask a sign for yourself from the LORD your God; ask it either in the depth or in the height above." 12 But Ahaz said, "I will not ask, nor will I test the LORD!" 13 Then he said, "Hear now, O house of David! Is it a small thing for you to weary men, but will you weary my God also? 14 "Therefore the Lord Himself will give you a sign: Behold, the virgin shall conceive and bear a Son, and shall call His name Immanuel.

Devotion

In this passage the Prophet Isaiah is speaking to one of the ruling descendants of David - King Ahaz. Ahaz had not chosen to honor God, and discipline was coming. Yet, God gave Ahaz a unique opportunity. Ahaz was given an opportunity to prove God by making any request that he wanted to prove that God still loved Israel, and that His ways were worth following. King Ahaz hid behind a cloak of personal piety claiming that he would not tempt the Lord. While the command not to test the Lord was certainly valid (according to Deuteronomy 6:16) this command did not apply in this situation because the Lord Himself was making this offer in order to change King Ahab's attitude and cause him to rule in obedience to God - which he had not been doing up to that point.

The Lord responds by telling King Ahab not to weary Him with these obfuscations and self-righteous posturing. Then the Lord tells Ahab what sign He would provide. The Lord refers to Ahab as "the house of David." While Ahab was the king in view, he was the representative of the entire house and line of David at that moment - as well as the promises which God had made to David. What sign would the Lord choose that the House of David would know that the Messiah had come?

The virgin would be with Child. We know that in order for a woman to become pregnant, especially given the technology available to them, it would be impossible that she should be a virgin. God promised that a virgin would give birth to a Child as a sign that this is God's will. Miraculous births were common in God's plan. Abraham and Sarah were not given their natural son Isaac until they were both past the years of their fertility and the potential for child bearing. Hannah had the same type of miraculous circumstance when bringing forth Samuel. In the New Testament Zechariah and Elizabeth would be under similar circumstances. But the miracle of the Birth of Jesus Christ was not simply a miraculous regeneration - or restoration of reproductive ability. Christ would come from Mary alone by the power of the Holy Spirit of God. This verse shows that virgin birth should have been understood in light of scripture and understood as the result of divine power in fulfillment of this specific prophecy.

DECEMBER 7TH

Isaiah 9:1-7

^{1} Nevertheless the gloom will not be upon her who is
distressed,
As when at first He lightly esteemed
The land of Zebulun and the land of Naphtali,
And afterward more heavily oppressed her,
By the way of the sea, beyond the Jordan,
In Galilee of the Gentiles.

^{2} The people who walked in darkness
Have seen a great light;
Those who dwelt in the land of the shadow of death,
Upon them a light has shined.
^{3} You have multiplied the nation
And increased its joy;
They rejoice before You
According to the joy of harvest,
As men rejoice when they divide the spoil.

^{4} For You have broken the yoke of his burden

And the staff of his shoulder,
The rod of his oppressor,
As in the day of Midian.
[5] For every warrior's sandal from the noisy battle,
And garments rolled in blood,
Will be used for burning and fuel of fire.

[6] For unto us a Child is born,
Unto us a Son is given;
And the government will be upon His shoulder.
And His name will be called Wonderful, Counselor,
Mighty God, Everlasting Father, Prince of Peace.
[7] Of the increase of His government and peace
There will be] no end,
Upon the throne of David and over His kingdom,
To order it and establish it with judgment and justice
From that time forward, even forever.
The zeal of the LORD of hosts will perform this.

Devotion

Like so many of the prophecies about the Ministry of Jesus Christ these the Old Testament prophets saw the events of the first coming and the second coming as being very close together. Sometimes, these prophets present these events in such close proximity that it is difficult to tell whether they are talking about Jesus first coming to pay for sin or His triumphant return to begin the Messianic Kingdom of God on Earth. Theologians call this "telescoping" which refers to the phenomenon that occurs when looking through a telescope at two stars or planets that may be separated by light-years, but look quite close in a telescope because of the angle at which we perceive them. The classic illustration of this is that the Old Testament prophets were seeing events like mountain peaks when looking across them from the perspective of another mountain peak. The "peak" of the first coming - the virgin birth to the crucifixion of the Messiah - looked very near indeed to the other peaks of the Tribulation and Antichrist, as well as the final peak of the Messianic reign.

This passage demonstrates this pattern in discussing many wonderful things about the Messianic Kingdom. Verses 1-5 of Isaiah 9 are discussing the joys, celebrations, and successes of the future reign of the Messiah. However, Isaiah 9:6 reverts to the ministry of Christ from the very beginning of his birth. "Unto us a Child is born" tells about the nature of the Messiah's birth. Like any other human being He spent around nine months growing and developing in Mary's womb. His body started as a small group of cells. Over time growing and developing a heartbeat, fingernails, eyes, and all of the other things that any baby would develop in the womb. Like all other human lives He would pass through the birth canal and draw His first breaths. This is an amazing reality to consider: Jesus Christ was fully human.

The phrase that completes this Hebrew poetry pattern completes the picture. "A Son is given." In His humanity, Jesus Christ was conceived of the Holy Spirit and born of the virgin Mary. However, He is given as the Eternal Son of God - the second member of the Trinity. As a child He was born, but as the Son He has always existed and always will exist - He is eternally the Son of God. Here we see the great paradox of the hypostatic union. Jesus Christ - fully God and fully human. His titles, given in verse seven highlight this same truth. The title Wonderful - speaks to the great and amazing nature of the Messiah's existence. The title Counselor of His infinite wisdom and the fact that in His Kingdom He will rule with all wisdom and knowledge. He alone has the ability and resources to make the best choices all the time.

The titles that follow speak yet more indisputably of the Messiah's deity. "Mighty God" is a phrase that could never be said of any mere mortal being. God is a jealous God and will not share His glory or His titles with anyone else - angelic or human. The Messiah, as we see, will be uniquely qualified to be called "Mighty God" without in any way taking glory from God the Father. This is what Philippians 2 means when it tells us that it was not robbery for Jesus to be considered equal to God - because He IS God in His very nature and essence.

The title "Everlasting Father" could be
translated as "Father of Eternity" or even "Father of
the Ages." The latter translations are preferred
because they help understand the difference between
the identity of God the Father and God the
Son. Jesus is, according to this title, the one who
created all of time and space as we know it. He is the
Father of all time and all of the rolling succession of
ages.

The final title: Prince of Peace speaks to the
nature of His reign. When the Messianic Kingdom
comes upon the earth it will be a time of peace and
prosperity unparalleled in all of human history. It will
be a time of great joy in which there will be no armed
conflict between the nations. No need to fight over
land, resources, or ideologies. Everything will be
perfectly provided by the Prince of Peace. The
account then continues to tell of the increase of His
government. His rule will have no end as He will rule
the entire world, and for the first time since the Fall
of Man, the World will be directly ruled by the Lord.

It is the zeal of the Lord that will give this gift
of the Christ, pay the price at the cross, and
administer this time to come on the
earth. Amazingly, we first encounter this Messiah in a
stable as a helpless infant in the care of a teenage
girl. That is the breathtaking reality of Who we
celebrate at Christmas.

DECEMBER 8ᵀᴴ

Isaiah 11:1-10

¹ There shall come forth a Rod from the stem of
Jesse,
And a Branch shall grow out of his roots.

² The Spirit of the LORD shall rest upon Him,
The Spirit of wisdom and understanding,
The Spirit of counsel and might,
The Spirit of knowledge and of the fear of the
LORD.
³ His delight is in the fear of the LORD,
And He shall not judge by the sight of His eyes,
Nor decide by the hearing of His ears;
⁴ But with righteousness He shall judge the poor,
And decide with equity for the meek of the earth;
He shall strike the earth with the rod of His mouth,
And with the breath of His lips He shall slay the
wicked.
⁵ Righteousness shall be the belt of His loins, And
faithfulness the belt of His waist.

[6] "The wolf also shall dwell with the lamb,
The leopard shall lie down with the young goat,
The calf and the young lion and the fatling together;
And a little child shall lead them.
[7] The cow and the bear shall graze;
Their young ones shall lie down together;
And the lion shall eat straw like the ox.
[8] The nursing child shall play by the cobra's hole,
And the weaned child shall put his hand in the viper's den.
[9] They shall not hurt nor destroy in all My holy mountain,
For the earth shall be full of the knowledge of the LORD
As the waters cover the sea.
[10] "And in that day there shall be a Root of Jesse,
Who shall stand as a banner to the people;
For the Gentiles shall seek Him,
And His resting place shall be glorious."

Devotion

These beautiful verses confirm the Davidic Covenant. "The Rod" again draws our thoughts to the Scepter of Jacob's prophetic words in Genesis 49, as well as the prophecy of Balaam. The Branch growing from the stem and root of Jesse relate the Messiah to the Davidic covenant. Jesse is King David's father. The use of both the Messiah being related to the branches of Jesse as well as the roots makes a clear statement that though the Messiah would be a physical descendant of Jesse, he is also the Jesse's creator.

Isaiah 11:2-5 reveals the character of the Messiah and His relationship to the Holy Spirit. The seven elements here are rightly alluded to later in the Book of Revelation as the "Seven-fold Spirit of God" (Revelation 1:4; 3:1; 4:5; 5:6). These elements are:

1 - The Spirit of the LORD - This is the Holy Spirit of God - the third Person of the Trinity.

2 - The Spirit of Wisdom - This is the Holy Spirit-enabled ability to always make the correct correlation and application of all of the facts.

3 - The Spirit of Understanding - This is the Holy Spirit's ministry to the Messiah by giving Him the perfect understanding of everything.

4 - The Spirit of Counsel - The Messiah will function in perfect harmony with the Holy Spirit to provide correct counsel in every situation.

5 - The Spirit of Might - This points us to the omnipotence of the Messiah. There is nothing that

he is unable to do.

6 - The Spirit of Knowledge - This tells of the omniscience of the Messiah - the Holy Spirit supplies Him with all knowledge and there is nothing that He does not know.

7 - The Spirit of the Fear of the LORD - The Spirit of the Fear or the LORD is not about a phobic fear, but a perfect and right relationship and respect to the other two members of the Trinity.

This perfect relationship of the Messiah to the Holy Spirit means that His reign will be perfect in all love, power, compassion, righteousness, and judgment. He will never "go wrong" or need to revise a decision. He will never act in haste, or lack the understanding or knowledge to make the best choice. Jesus Christ, whose earthly entrance we celebrate at Christmas, is perfectly qualified to make good on every promise of God because He is perfectly and infinitely qualified.

Isaiah 11:6-11 describes the conditions of the Messianic Kingdom. The conditions of peace and harmony are wondrous to consider. There will no longer be any danger from or between animals that are predators in this age. There will be peace in the natural world as well as in the world of human affairs. This is all possible only because of the character of the Messiah. This future will exist on this Earth under the righteous reign of Jesus Christ because He alone was qualified to pay the penalty for sin at the Cross. At Christmas we celebrate the Earth's introduction to the only One who would pay the penalty and bring redemption and salvation to lost sinners - US! We receive that gift by faith in His perfect Person and work.

DECEMBER 9TH

Isaiah 53

[1]Who has believed our report?
And to whom has the arm of the LORD been
revealed?
[2]For He shall grow up before Him as a tender plant,
And as a root out of dry ground.

He has no form or comeliness;
And when we see Him,
There is no beauty that we should desire Him.
[3]He is despised and rejected by men,
A Man of sorrows and acquainted with grief.
And we hid, as it were, our faces from Him;
He was despised, and we did not esteem Him.

[4]Surely He has borne our griefs
And carried our sorrows;
Yet we esteemed Him stricken,
Smitten by God, and afflicted.
[5]But He was wounded for our transgressions,

He was bruised for our iniquities;
The chastisement for our peace was upon Him,
And by His stripes we are healed.
⁶All we like sheep have gone astray;
We have turned, every one, to his own way;
And the LORD has laid on Him the iniquity of us all.

⁷ He was oppressed and He was afflicted,
Yet He opened not His mouth;
He was led as a lamb to the slaughter,
And as a sheep before its shearers is silent,
So He opened not His mouth.
⁸He was taken from prison and from judgment,
And who will declare His generation?
For He was cut off from the land of the living;
For the transgressions of My people He was stricken.
⁹And they made His grave with the wicked—
But with the rich at His death,
Because He had done no violence,
Nor was any deceit in His mouth.

¹⁰Yet it pleased the LORD to bruise Him;
He has put Him to grief.
When You make His soul an offering for sin,
He shall see His seed,
He shall prolong His days,
And the pleasure of the LORD shall prosper in His hand.

¹¹He shall see the labor of His soul, and be satisfied.
By His knowledge My righteous Servant shall justify many,
For He shall bear their iniquities.

[12]Therefore I will divide Him a portion with the great,
And He shall divide the spoil with the strong,
Because He poured out His soul unto death,
And He was numbered with the transgressors,
And He bore the sin of many,
And made intercession for the transgressors."

Devotion

This passage is not usually associated with Christmas time. This clear prophecy about the Cross of Jesus Christ is often reserved for celebrations of Passover and Resurrection Sunday. Yet, our celebration of Christmas would be incomplete if we did not consider the mission which Jesus Christ came to the earth to fulfill. The issue of paying for sin. The Jewish people were perplexed at these two pictures of Messiah. The Messiah's reign was to be a time of peace and blessing upon the earth that would last forever. Yet, passages like Isaiah 53 and Psalm 22 predicted a suffering Messiah who would pay the price for sin.

Many Jewish Bible interpreters could not imagine how these two disparate Messianic figures could both be the same person. They came to the conclusion that if Israel continued in sin and rebellion against God that the suffering Messiah would have to come to pay for the sins of Israel. However, if Israel was found in faithfulness then they could expect the triumphant ruling Messiah who would rule over the world in peace and justice. They came to this conclusion because they did not yet understand the pervasive and incurable evil of sin.

Isaiah 53 paints a picture of the Messiah which we now see clearly. The sin problem had to be dealt with completely. Man's just punishment of death and eternal separation from God who is holy and righteous had to be resolved. The Messiah's first coming paid the eternal penalty for sin. The substitutionary death of the Messiah is mentioned at least 14 times in these twelve verses. The Messiah would come and bear the penalty of sin. Not only the sins of Israel, but the sins of the entire world. Because Jesus Christ came as "the Lamb of God who takes away the sins of the world" (John 1:29) salvation is offered to all men who receive that precious gift by faith in Jesus Christ.

DECEMBER 10TH

Daniel 9:22-27

22 And he informed me, and talked with me, and said,

"O Daniel, I have now come forth to give you skill to understand.
23 At the beginning of your supplications the command went out, and I have come to tell you, for you are greatly beloved; therefore consider the matter, and understand the vision:

24 "Seventy weeks are determined
For your people and for your holy city,
To finish the transgression,
To make an end of sins,
To make reconciliation for iniquity,

To bring in everlasting righteousness,
To seal up vision and prophecy,
And to anoint the Most Holy.

25"Know therefore and understand,
That from the going forth of the command
To restore and build Jerusalem Until Messiah
the Prince,
There shall be seven weeks and sixty-two
weeks;
The street shall be built again, and the wall,
Even in troublesome times.

26"And after the sixty-two weeks Messiah shall
be cut off, but not for Himself;
And the people of the prince who is to come
Shall destroy the city and the sanctuary.
The end of it shall be with a flood,
And till the end of the war desolations are
determined.
27 Then he shall confirm a covenant with
many for one week;
But in the middle of the week He shall bring
an end to sacrifice and offering.
And on the wing of abominations shall be one
who makes desolate,
Even until the consummation, which is
determined,
Is poured out on the desolate."

Devotion

Daniel is a very special Old Testament prophet. As a young man, Daniel was taken captive by King Nebuchadnezzar of Babylon along with his friends Shadrach, Meshech, and Abednego. They were taken to Babylon when Nebuchadnezzar conquered the southern Kingdom of Judah. It was Babylon's way to take the best and brightest young men from any conquered territory to educate them in the Babylonian way of life to help bring the conquered nation under obedience to the empire. Daniel quickly rose to prominence as a result of his God-given wisdom and ability to interpret dreams. He was given the interpretation of Nebuchadnezzar's dream of a great statue that was used to portray the coming great empires of the ancient world - Babylon, Medo-Persia, Greece, and Rome. This vision caused Nebuchadnezzar to show reverence for the God of Israel. It also provided important information about the timeline of the Lord's plan for the ages.

Later in life, Daniel was given more revelation about that timing that was more specific. This is sometimes known as Daniel's prophecy of the 70 weeks. The word translated "weeks" can cause some confusion for the modern reader. It translates the Hebrew word that is literally the number seven. Since the creation of the world seven is a number that is used to mark time. Seven days is a complete week, and every seven years the Jews were to celebrate a Sabbath year where the land was to rest from planting and harvesting. Every seven sets of seven years (49 years) there was to be a celebration called the Year of

Jubilee. During the year of Jubilee property would return to its ancestral owners, slaves would go free, and debts would be forgiven. Furthermore, when Jacob served Laban for the right to marry Laban's daughters, seven years was considered a natural amount of time to make a full payment. Each of these is an important "seven". Because of the relationship between a "seven" and what we now call a week, translators brought this concept into English as "seventy weeks" rather than the more literal "seventy sevens". This is understandable for ease of reading, but makes it more difficult to understand that the prophecy given to Daniel was not seventy sets of seven days (weeks of days) but rather seventy sets of seven years (weeks of years). This meant that there would be 490 years to complete God's entire prophetic plan on the earth and bring about Messiah's kingdom. Yet something remarkable would happen prior to that final set of seven years. The Messiah would come on to the scene.

This is an important timing indicator for the first coming of Messiah. In brief, those 69 weeks of years (483 years) brings us to AD 29/30 which is the beginning of Jesus' public ministry on the earth. This means that Jesus had to be born in a time that would bring him to adulthood and preparation to begin his earthly ministry by that time. There are several ways in which this could work out, and scholars have written much, but it makes a comfortable fit with the traditional date of Jesus Christ's birth on or around 4 BC. Jesus came at just the right time to fulfill all of the Messianic prophecies and promises that were set out for Him. Yet, this important prophecy has even more to tell us about the earthly ministry of Jesus Christ.

We are told that the Messiah would be cut off. This is a prophecy of Jesus Christ's death and payment for sin. Having been crucified, the Romans (the people of the prince who is to come - the Antichrist) would destroy Jerusalem in 70 ad. This leads into a period of parenthesis until the rebuilding of the temple, the revelation of the Antichrist, who will make a 7-year peace treaty with the nation of Israel. At the mid-point of this period of devastation the Antichrist will break the treaty with Israel and put a stop to temple worship. This period ends with the great war described in Zechariah 14 and Revelation 19.

The Church, as a mystery unseen by the Old Testament prophets, will be taken up to be with Jesus before this time of judgment upon the earth that will bring the nation of Israel back to faith in God through the Messiah, Jesus Christ. The message for this Christmas, and every day, is that God is sovereign over all of human history and it will bring His full plan of redemption for the earth to bear in His time and to His glory. We celebrate His great faithfulness and perfect plan each year when we celebrate the key moment when Jesus Christ took on full humanity and identified with us so that salvation could be offered to all, freely by His grace, before His plan is fulfilled upon the earth in His glorious future Kingdom.

The Gift of Christmas

DECEMBER 11ᵀᴴ

Micah 5:2

"But you, Bethlehem Ephrathah,
Though you are little among the thousands of Judah,
Yet out of you shall come forth to Me
The One to be Ruler in Israel,
Whose goings forth are from of old,
From everlasting."

Devotion

This prophecy was given by the prophet Micah to the Kingdom of Judah. Micah was a contemporary of Isaiah and was given some key information on the theme of the Messiah as well. In this case, a location is given. Bethlehem Ephrathah is the ancestral home of David. This means that the prophecy actually would have made a great deal of sense to the original recipients. From the modern perspective we may be tempted to think that the Lord selected a city at random. However, given the Messianic aspect of the Davidic covenant this would be the city that one would expect to see the Messiah enter our world. This takes nothing from the miraculous nature of the prophecy, in fact it amplifies it! By the time that the Messiah would come the line of David had been scattered and the true Davidic heir (Joseph) was not living in Bethlehem. God moved human governments to bring about the fulfillment of this prophecy.

The name of the city also holds significance. The word Bethlehem is a compound word adding the word for "house" to the word for "bread." Bethlehem could literally be translated as "House of Bread." This is very appropriate given that Jesus Christ - the Bread of Life (John 6:35) - would come to the city of Bethlehem. This prophecy highlights the miraculous and amazing plan of God. But this passage has more to tell us about the Messiah, our Savior.

This One coming forth will be a ruler in Israel. The specific relationship of the Messiah to the nation of Israel is plain. There is no way one can talk about the Messiah of the Old Testament without also recognizing that His mission was to be the literal ruler in the nation of Israel. Micah 5:2 also reveals something about the origin of the Messiah: His eternality. His coming and going was from "of old." This idiomatic phrase explains that the Messiah wouldn't start when He entered the scene. He would exist before the time people saw him. The phrase "from of old" makes it clear that this Messiah was active long before Micah's ministry as well. This speaks to the supernatural character and nature of the Messiah.

The last statement absolutely solidifies the thought for the attentive audience: He is from everlasting. The idea of being from a specific time or place is reasonable for us to understand. But to be from everlasting? From Eternity? The origin of the Messiah would be outside of time and space as we understand it. This is a clear statement of what happened on that Christmas morning: The Son of God - wholly divine - took on human flesh. He stepped out of eternity to be uniquely present in the time which He created. Because Jesus Christ entered into our world we now have access to Him - personally and intimately. Not only would He come to us, but because He identified with us, the way was open for the Father to identify us with Him. So we are identified with Jesus Christ in death, burial, resurrection, ascension, and seating. All because of what happened on that day we celebrate each year at Christmas.

DECEMBER 12ᵀᴴ

Matthew 2:1-12

¹Now after Jesus was born in Bethlehem of Judea in the days of Herod the king, behold, wise men from the East came to Jerusalem, ²saying, "Where is He who has been born King of the Jews? For we have seen His star in the East and have come to worship Him."

³ When Herod the king heard this, he was troubled, and all Jerusalem with him. ⁴And when he had gathered all the chief priests and scribes of the people together, he inquired of them where the Christ was to be born. ⁵So they said to him, "In Bethlehem of Judea, for thus it is written by the prophet:
⁶'But you, Bethlehem, in the land of Judah,
Are not the least among the rulers of Judah;
For out of you shall come a Ruler
Who will shepherd My people Israel.' "

⁷Then Herod, when he had secretly called the wise

men, determined from them what time the star appeared. [8]And he sent them to Bethlehem and said, "Go and search carefully for the young Child, and when you have found Him, bring back word to me, that I may come and worship Him also."

[9]When they heard the king, they departed; and behold, the star which they had seen in the East went before them, till it came and stood over where the young Child was. [10]When they saw the star, they rejoiced with exceedingly great joy. [11]And when they had come into the house, they saw the young Child with Mary His mother, and fell down and worshiped Him. And when they had opened their treasures, they presented gifts to Him: gold, frankincense, and myrrh. [12]Then, being divinely warned in a dream that they should not return to Herod, they departed for their own country another way.

Devotion

In the traditional church calendar this passage is not considered until what is called Epiphany. This is owing to the fact that the visit of the Magi (the Wisemen from the east) was likely as much as two years after the event of Jesus Christ's birth. These Wisemen have been associated with kings based upon Psalm 72:11 which says:

Yes, all kings shall fall down before Him; All nations shall serve Him.

Not fully understanding the distinction between the first and second comings of the Messiah caused early church leaders to think that these magi must be kings in fulfillment of this prophetic Psalm. However, this prophecy will be fulfilled at the Second Coming in the Messiah's kingdom.

So if they weren't kings, who were they? The answer to this question relies upon the book of Daniel. Daniel was taken captive by Babylon and over the course of his life rose to the very highest ranks among the wisemen who would serve as counselors to the king. Daniel served in this capacity through the end of the Babylonian empire and into the Persian empire. He and other Jewish scholars continued to have places among the wisemen bringing the wisdom of God's words and all of the prophetic promises of the coming Messiah. One important prophecy that they remembered was the prophecy of Balaam recorded in Numbers 24:17. This prophecy spoke of a great ruler that would come forth from Israel at the appropriate time who was referred to as a "star."

These wise men kept this prophecy in mind as they paid close attention to the movement of the stars. Upon the birth of Jesus, they saw a special phenomenon in the sky which they identified with this Messianic promise and they came to recognize the coming King who would come forth from Israel.

Because of the number of gifts they brought, early Christians assumed they must be three in number. However, it is more likely that it was a great band of them, along with attendants, to recognize the new King. These "king-makers" from the east would surely be of notice to Herod - the insecure Edomite ruler who had connived his way to the heights of the Roman political system - to wrongfully take on the Messianic title "the King of the Jews."

Thus, Herod, filled with deadly and Satanic rage, would use this information to try and end the life of this threat to his illegitimate throne by killing all of the young people in Bethlehem. Herod surely did not know that he was taking part in the universal spiritual war of Satan against God's promised coming Messiah. God revealed that danger to the Holy Family and they were saved by fleeing to Egypt.

These Magi brought gifts to the King. The gift of gold was fitting and worthy of a king and foreshadows the abundance and wealth of His coming reign upon the earth. The gift of frankincense alluded to the priestly nature of the Messiah's reign. The Messiah would not be simply a political power, but would also be the access point between man and God. Myrrh was a spice used to embalm the dead. This gift alluded to the coming death of the Messiah to pay for the sins of the world. Each of these gifts gives the indication that the Wisemen from the east recognized the prophetic significance of this Child born in Bethlehem. Each Christmas season we are blessed to consider the gift of the Savior - Prophet, Priest, and King.

The Gift of Christmas

DECEMBER 13TH

Philippians 2:1-11

⁵Let this mind be in you which was also in Christ Jesus, ⁶who, being in the form of God, did not consider it robbery to be equal with God, ⁷but made Himself of no reputation, taking the form of a bondservant, and coming in the likeness of men.

⁸And being found in appearance as a man, He humbled Himself and became obedient to the point of death, even the death of the cross.

⁹Therefore God also has highly exalted Him and given Him the name which is above every name, ¹⁰that at the name of Jesus every knee should bow, of those in heaven, and of those on earth, and of those under the earth, ¹¹and that every tongue should confess that Jesus Christ is Lord, to the glory of God the Father.

Devotion

We generally look down upon condescending people. However, Philippians 2 gives us a powerful explanation of the meaning and importance of Christmas. We love to see a celebrity visiting a terminally ill child who happens to be a fan of theirs. The celebrity comes from a place of wealth, prestige, and power and the child is nearly hopeless and helpless in their affliction. The idea that the greatest would take time to encourage the least is something that we are built to appreciate. However, in the case of the celebrity visiting the child, the differences are only superficial. While they are in very different situations in the material world - both are simply sinful, lost, and hopeless people who need the saving work of Jesus Christ. The condescension is not so dramatic as it may at first appear.

Philippians chapter 2 gives us a view of the greatest condescension that ever occurred. When Jesus Christ - who is equal to God the Father in nature, essence, and power - took on human flesh - the angelic world surely stopped in awe and wonder. The One who created all things entered into His creation? The one who designed all of the confines of reality would now allow Himself to be confined by it. This consideration is surely too great for our full appreciation, but it brings us to a place of understanding what humility truly means.

The God of the Universe had to learn to walk, talk, change clothes, and sleep. It is difficult to imagine. A teenage girl carried the Son of God to term. Fed Him with her body, which He had created, and depended upon her for every physical thing. As we sit in amazement at what this means we are truly understanding the miracle of the Christmas season. The great condescension did not end there. He would not rise immediately to His place of obvious power and authority in the world of men. He was rejected, humiliated, and died a criminal's death. This action became the universal definition of "humility" in a single action.

This humility of Christ causes us to explode into worship. Not only humans, but also the rest of all the world of God's creation - seen and unseen. The angelic assembly that announced the Messiah's birth to the shepherds were privileged indeed. The Glorified Christ as we will behold Him in His Kingdom will give us that opportunity to sing His praises for all eternity. The best news? We need not wait! This Christmas we can turn all of our focus upon the Son of God who came to earth to save us.

The Gift of Christmas

DECEMBER 14TH

Galatians 4:1-7

[1]Now I say that the heir, as long as he is a child, does not differ at all from a slave, though he is master of all, [2]but is under guardians and stewards until the time appointed by the father. [3]Even so we, when we were children, were in bondage under the elements of the world. [4]But when the fullness of the time had come, God sent forth His Son, born of a woman, born under the law, [5]to redeem those who were under the law, that we might receive the adoption as sons.

[6]And because you are sons, God has sent forth the Spirit of His Son into your hearts, crying out, "Abba, Father!" [7]Therefore you are no longer a slave but a son, and if a son, then an heir of God through Christ.

Devotion

In the Book of Galatians Paul is dealing with a very serious problem. The church in the region of Galatia had trusted in Jesus Christ and His work upon the cross for salvation. Then the deceivers moved in behind Paul and told these young believers that, though they were saved by the grace of God initially, they must continue on by their own works. They were hoping to place these young believers under the Law of Moses.

Paul explodes with revulsion and anger. Our justification and our growth come by the grace gifting of God and not by works lest any man should boast. By making the work of Christ a "little help", instead of our complete salvation, they lost completely any chance of knowing Christ or understanding Christ and the Salvation He has given us. Galatians is a serious book.

While defending these vital themes Galatians 4:4 stands out. The fullness of time is an expression that could easily be translated as as "when the time was right." The imagery, however, is more powerful than that. The idea of the fullness of time draws to the mind a pregnant woman on the final day of her pregnancy. The child is big and ready and has moved down into position for the birth. She feels the pressure on her hips, as she has for weeks, and cannot walk easily but falls into the "pregnant lady waddle." She is ready to deliver her child. All of the discomfort, fear, and anticipation is coming to a big moment and, at the end, she will get to meet the new baby. That is the picture of "the fullness of times." Jesus came to the earth at exactly the right moment.

In what ways is this the case? First, He came in perfect keeping with the timing prophecies of Daniel. God's plan for the nations had clearly been laid out, and it was time for the Messiah to enter the scene. The prophecies of the seventy-sevens - the period of 490 years prophesied in Daniel 9:27 - had come to their fulfillment and the time had come to see the Messiah enter the scene. Not only that the world was prepared. The conquest of Alexander the Great brought Hellenism - Greek culture - to the entire known world. For the first time since the Tower of Babel there was one language (Koine Greek) that would be useful almost all over the world. This means that the New Testament could be given in a single common language and understood by all. Previous eras of military conflict and struggle had been quelled in the famous Pax Romana (the Peace of Rome). This peace meant that the appearance of Christ would not be obscured by any external military conflicts. Not only this, Roman roads provided the best system for safe and effective travel that the world had ever seen. God's plan has taken thousands of years to unfold, and with each turn it becomes increasingly apparent that His plan is perfect.

The Son of God came into the world born of a woman, living a life under the law - the only person to ever perfectly fulfill the Law of Moses and be declared absolutely righteous by its standard. The result of the perfect timing of this mission was the perfect fulfillment of the Messianic hope. Sinful and fallen mankind can be redeemed. This redemption is offered to us and now, because of what God has done through Jesus Christ we can be bought back and brought back into the family of God. Where He was once our enemy, He is now our Father - personally and individually. All because of the miracle we celebrate on Christmas day.

DECEMBER 15TH

Hosea 11:1

"When Israel was a child, I loved him,
And out of Egypt I called My son."

Devotion

Of all the prophets of the Old Testament the book of Hosea may offer the most dramatic illustration of the Lord's great love for Israel. The prophet Hosea was employed by God as a living illustration of Israel's unfaithfulness to God, and His unending faithfulness to pursue His chosen earthly people. The manner of this living illustration was most painful for the prophet Hosea. He was commanded by God to take a wife named Gomer who proved to be unfaithful. Time and time again she betrayed him and sold herself back into slavery and prostitution. Each time he lovingly bought her back - purchasing her out of her captivity and raising the children of her infidelity.

This vivid picture in the life of Hosea brings about strong feelings in the audience. How could Gomer be unfaithful to a husband who provided so much? How could Hosea show love and grace for one who had publicly humiliated and rejected him? Yet, this powerful story was an illustration of the Lord's great love for the nation of Israel. He had chosen Abraham out of an idolatrous and God-rejecting culture. He had redeemed the nation of Israel from her slavery in Egypt. God had been faithful to keep and redeem them throughout the periods of the Judges by raising up leaders to redeem them when their sins had led them to be occupied by foreign powers. His faithfulness had persisted in spite of their constant return to worship the various false gods. Again and again, they rejected them and experienced the consequences. He always lovingly called them back to Himself and redeemed them.

This prophecy was fulfilled in Matthew 2:13-

23. The murderous rage of Herod caused the holy family to flee Israel and find safety in Egypt, likely staying in one of the Jewish communities that dwelt there. This relates Jesus to the love story that God told through Hosea as Jesus is the fulfillment of all of the promises made through Hosea and all of the prophets. Sin pushed God's Anointed One out of the land. Just as God had called captive Israel out of bondage in Egypt so God would call His Son, Jesus Christ, out of Egypt and into the land. Jesus is the fulfillment of God's forever-love and faithfulness to Israel and to all of humanity. When it came to redeeming sinful man, in spite of endless rejection and rebellion, God paid the ultimate price by sending His only Son, Jesus Christ to bring us back to Him. In the end, He will show that in Christ all of His promises are fulfilled and His plan will be brought forth to His glory.

The Gift of Christmas

DECEMBER 16ᵀᴴ

Hebrews 1:1-4

¹God, who at various times and in various ways spoke in time past to the fathers by the prophets, ²has in these last days spoken to us by His Son, whom He has appointed heir of all things, through whom also He made the worlds; ³who being the brightness of His glory and the express image of His person, and upholding all things by the word of His power, when He had by Himself purged our sins, sat down at the right hand of the Majesty on high, ⁴having become so much better than the angels, as He has by inheritance

obtained a more excellent name than they.

Colossians 1:15-18

[15]He is the image of the invisible God, the firstborn over all creation. [16]For by Him all things were created that are in heaven and that are on earth, visible and invisible, whether thrones or dominions or principalities or powers. All things were created through Him and for Him. [17]And He is before all things, and in Him all things consist. 18 And He is the head of the body, the church, who is the beginning, the firstborn from the dead, that in all things He may have the preeminence.

Devotion

What do we celebrate at Christmas? For some it is about the decorations. For others the fun of giving and receiving gifts. Most will enjoy time with family and friends at various parties, programs and gatherings. Christmas would be wasted, however, if we failed to consider the immensity of the miracle that occurred when God became a man. The Second Person of the Triune God took on flesh and lived with us. This is an event so extraordinary that it merits our constant amazement.

The author of Hebrews reminds early Jewish believers that Jesus Christ is the best. Better than angels, Moses, Tabernacle worship, the Old Testament Law and Priesthood...everything! Jesus Christ is the ultimate revelation of God to mankind - the clearest picture that we could ever have to understand Him. Being in very nature God, Jesus Christ stepped down into our world to show us Who He is in ways that we could understand.

Relating to God may seem abstract. To be close to God who is perfect in His holiness, justice, righteousness, and truth would be simply impossible for us in our sinfulness. This is why Jesus came down to meet us in our place of helplessness and need. He became a human being that people could approach, question, listen to, and see. He showed us love that we could see and understand. He displayed the passionate heart of God to seek and save that which was lost. He laid down His life that we could be cleansed and forgiven and restored to the God from whom we had wandered and strayed.

In Colossians 1:15-18 the Apostle Paul conveys much the same message to an audience of believers who were predominantly Gentile. Both passages affirm the divinity of Jesus. Jesus is the major Agent of Creation. This world was made by Him and for Him. At Christmas we celebrate the fact that in Jesus Christ we can see and know the God of the Universe. In the Church we are His body - related to Him in absolute unity and eternal identification. Here to do His will and represent Him upon the earth.

This is only possible because He came to earth as an infant some 2,000 years ago. Because of Christmas we can know God. Not as a set of theological dogmas, nor as a matter of intellectual understanding - but personally, relationally, intimately. We can enjoy the personal relationship with God that we were created to have because He came to us in a way that was personal. Christmas is a time of ultimate joy and celebration.

DECEMBER 17TH

Romans 5:12-21

[12]Therefore, just as through one man sin entered the world, and death through sin, and thus death spread to all men, because all sinned-- [13](For until the law sin was in the world, but sin is not imputed when there is no law. [14]Nevertheless death reigned from Adam to Moses, even over those who had not sinned according to the likeness of the transgression of Adam, who is a type of Him who was to come. [15]But the free gift is not like the offense. For if by the one man's offense many died, much more the grace of God and the gift by the grace of the one Man, Jesus Christ, abounded to many.

[16]And the gift is not like that which came through the one who sinned. For the judgment which came from one offense resulted in condemnation, but the free gift which came from many offenses resulted in justification. [17]For if by the one man's offense death reigned through the one, much more those who

receive abundance of grace and of the gift of righteousness will reign in life through the One, Jesus Christ.)

[18]Therefore, as through one man's offense judgment came to all men, resulting in condemnation, even so through one Man's righteous act the free gift came to all men, resulting in justification of life. [19]For as by one man's disobedience many were made sinners, so also by one Man's obedience many will be made righteous.

[20]Moreover the law entered that the offense might abound. But where sin abounded, grace abounded much more, [21]so that as sin reigned in death, even so grace might reign through righteousness to eternal life through Jesus Christ our Lord.

Devotion

We tend to take birth for granted. Since birth has been the way that every human has entered this world since Adam and Eve we very seldom spend much time thinking about all that it entails. Yet, birth is God's method of Creation. When God created Adam and Eve He also created every single person that would be born of them and their descendants. That initial creative act of making Adam and Eve was the starting point for bringing forth all of the people that came forth afterwards - including you and me! God started a process in the first week of creation that continues on to this day.

The reality of birth grows ever more amazing upon continued scrutiny. It connects all humans to one another. Not one person arrives on this planet on their own - they all had to be born into this world by the continuation of that creative act of God. In this way we all share identity together. Children are born with the features and traits of their parents because they share a federal headship in their parents. All of the families on earth trace their way surely back through their various lineages to our federal head: Adam.

Adam was created in the very image of God. A finite version of God designed to be God's steward over all of the world that the Lord had created. Sin, as we know, marred that image. The destiny of our federal head Adam changed when Adam and Eve sinned and thus the destiny of every one of his descendants changed as well. When Adam rebelled and died spiritually everyone who would be born of him would likewise be spiritually dead. What seemed to be a problem for Adam was actually a problem for everyone who would proceed forth from Adam. Yet, God's solution was contained in the very problem.

Our condemnation was related to the condemnation of Adam. Yet, because of how God created us to exist in relationship to a federal head. He needed to provide a new federal head to provide salvation. God provided for us a new federal head in Jesus Christ. Born of a Virgin he was not a part of Adam's line and therefore did not receive Adam's destiny. He became for us a new head. When we trust in Jesus Christ we are removed from the condemned line of Adam by God's sovereign hand and placed into the new line of Christ. We are made new creatures and are eternally and fundamentally changed. From death to life, from hopelessness to hope, from hatred to love. We are now connected to the righteous line of Jesus Christ - all because God created us through His special means of human birth. That makes the Birth that we celebrate at Christmas a greater thing than we can ever fully appreciate.

DECEMBER 18TH

Matthew 1:1-17

¹The book of the genealogy of Jesus Christ, the Son of David, the Son of Abraham: ²Abraham begot Isaac, Isaac begot Jacob, and Jacob begot Judah and his brothers. ³Judah begot Perez and Zerah by Tamar, Perez begot Hezron, and Hezron begot Ram. ⁴Ram begot Amminadab, Amminadab begot Nahshon, and Nahshon begot Salmon. ⁵Salmon begot Boaz by Rahab, Boaz begot Obed by Ruth, Obed begot Jesse, ⁶and Jesse begot David the king. David the king begot Solomon by her [who had been the wife] of Uriah. ⁷Solomon begot Rehoboam, Rehoboam begot Abijah, and Abijah begot Asa. ⁸Asa begot Jehoshaphat, Jehoshaphat begot Joram, and Joram begot Uzziah. ⁹Uzziah begot Jotham, Jotham begot Ahaz, and Ahaz begot Hezekiah. ¹⁰Hezekiah begot Manasseh, Manasseh begot Amon, and Amon begot Josiah. ¹¹Josiah begot Jeconiah and his brothers about the time they were carried away to Babylon. ¹²And after they were brought to Babylon, Jeconiah begot

Shealtiel, and Shealtiel begot Zerubbabel.
[13]Zerubbabel begot Abiud, Abiud begot Eliakim, and
Eliakim begot Azor. [14]Azor begot Zadok, Zadok
begot Achim, and Achim begot Eliud. [15]Eliud begot
Eleazar, Eleazar begot Matthan, and Matthan begot
Jacob. [16]And Jacob begot Joseph the husband of
Mary, of whom was born Jesus who is called Christ. [17]
So all the generations from Abraham to David are
fourteen generations, from David until the captivity in
Babylon are fourteen generations, and from the
captivity in Babylon until the Christ are fourteen
generations.

Luke 3:23-38

[23]Now Jesus Himself began His ministry at about
thirty years of age, being (as was supposed) the son of
Joseph, the son of Heli, [24]the son of Matthat, the son
of Levi, the son of Melchi, the son of Janna, the son
of Joseph, [25]the son of Mattathiah, the son of Amos,
the son of Nahum, the son of Esli, the son of Naggai,
[26]the son of Maath, the son of Mattathiah, the son of
Semei, the son of Joseph, the son of Judah, [27]the son
of Joannas, the son of Rhesa, the son of Zerubbabel,
the son of Shealtiel, the son of Neri, [28]the son of
Melchi, the son of Addi, the son of Cosam, the son of
Elmodam, the son of Er, [29]the son of Jose, the son of
Eliezer, the son of Jorim, the son of Matthat, the son
of Levi, [30]the son of Simeon, the son of Judah, the
son of Joseph, the son of Jonan, the son of Eliakim,
[31]the son of Melea, the son of Menan, the son of
Mattathah, the son of Nathan, the son of David, [32]the
son of Jesse, the son of Obed, the son of Boaz, the
son of Salmon, the son of Nahshon, [33]the son of
Amminadab, the son of Ram, the son of Hezron, the

son of Perez, the son of Judah, ³⁴the son of Jacob, the
son of Isaac, the son of Abraham, the son of Terah,
the son of Nahor, ³⁵the son of Serug, the son of Reu,
the son of Peleg, the son of Eber, the son of Shelah,
³⁶ [the son] of Cainan, the son of Arphaxad, the son
of Shem, the son of Noah, the son of Lamech, ³⁷the
son of Methuselah, the son of Enoch, the son of
Jared, the son of Mahalalel, the son of Cainan, ³⁸the
son of Enosh, the son of Seth, the son of Adam, the
son of God.

Devotion

Of the four accounts of the life of Jesus
Christ in Matthew, Mark, Luke, and John. Only two
of them contain genealogies. This may seem
unnecessary from a modern perspective, but both of
these accounts of the lineage of Jesus Christ are
important. They relate Jesus to the Messianic
promises and prophecies. They certify that He is the
One who is qualified to come and save the world.

Both genealogies relate Jesus to David, to the
Tribe of Judah, and finally to Abraham. Luke's
account goes yet further to relate Jesus to Adam. The
reason for this difference is significant. Matthew
wrote with the purpose of showing the nation of
Israel that Jesus was their Messiah. Thus, it was
reasonable for his account to stop at Abraham who
was chosen by God to be the beginning of the nation
of Israel. Luke, however, had a gentile audience in
mind and thus showed that Jesus' line went all the
way back to Adam - we all share a common
ancestor. Jesus Christ came as king of the Jews and
He also came to be Savior of the World.

The complications and differences in the two
accounts have caused consternation to many Bible
students and yet there are some important
considerations that we must understand. First, both
Matthew and Luke would have had access to the
records that were contained in the Temple in
Jerusalem. That meant that they were able to pore
over the accurate records which the Jewish people
kept of their lineages. All of these records were
destroyed at the 70 AD destruction of the
Temple. This is a tragedy, yet it shows that these

documents, when written, were very well researched and could be confirmed or denied by anyone who had access to the temple. This means that these records withstood the scrutiny and attack of those who rejected Jesus as the Messiah and would have found it easy to debunk His authenticity simply by producing records that would contradict the accounts assembled by Matthew and Luke. History provides us with no examples of any such attack on the reliability of these important New Testament records. This gives us confidence in the lineage of the Messiah.

How do we account for the apparent differences? A few facts alleviate any concern about the differences between these passages. In the keeping of ancient genealogies, it was very common to skip generations. In fact, language scholars now agree that "descendant of" would be a better translation than "son of" - and Luke leaves those words out altogether simply listing important people in the line of Jesus in chronicle order. Another important point is that of Levirate marriage which is commanded in Deuteronomy 25:5-6. This process was put in place by God so that the name and legal inheritance would be preserved even if a person were to die childless. If a man died without an heir, his widow would marry his brother and the child born into that union would be the legal heir of the dead brother, but the biological child of the living brother. These marriages can thus provide two genealogies - one biological and one legal. Adoption can also play an important role in much the same manner.

One final possible relief to the apparent tension is in the question of whether Luke and

Matthew were both pursuing different genealogies - Matthew from the perspective of tracing Jesus' legal line in light of His adoption by Joseph and Luke tracing His biological line through His mother Mary. This is especially important because it protects Jesus from the Jechonian curse. Jeremiah 22:24 and 30 record a curse laid upon the rebellious king Jechoniah that none from his genetic line should be king of Israel. Yet, as Jesus is adopted into this line, He is still qualified to be King and is not subject to that curse. Additionally, the fact that He is also of the Davidic line through the lineage of Mary He is singularly and perfectly qualified to be the Messiah: The King of the Jews and the Savior of All who would believe in Him.

DECEMBER 19ᵀᴴ

Luke 1:5-25

⁵ There was in the days of Herod, the king of Judea, a certain priest named Zacharias, of the division of Abijah. His wife was of the daughters of Aaron, and her name was Elizabeth. ⁶ And they were both righteous before God, walking in all the commandments and ordinances of the Lord blameless. ⁷ But they had no child, because Elizabeth was barren, and they were both well advanced in years. ⁸ So it was, that while he was serving as priest before God in the order of his division, ⁹ according to the custom of the priesthood, his lot fell to burn incense when he went into the temple of the Lord. ¹⁰ And the whole multitude of the people was praying outside at the hour of incense. ¹¹ Then an angel of the Lord appeared to him, standing on the right side of the altar of incense. ¹² And when Zacharias saw him, he was troubled, and fear fell upon him. ¹³ But the angel said to him, "Do not be afraid, Zacharias, for your prayer is heard; and your wife Elizabeth will bear

you a son, and you shall call his name John. [14] "And you will have joy and gladness, and many will rejoice at his birth. [15] "For he will be great in the sight of the Lord, and shall drink neither wine nor strong drink. He will also be filled with the Holy Spirit, even from his mother's womb. [16] "And he will turn many of the children of Israel to the Lord their God. [17] "He will also go before Him in the spirit and power of Elijah, 'to turn the hearts of the fathers to the children,' and the disobedient to the wisdom of the just, to make ready a people prepared for the Lord." [18] And Zacharias said to the angel, "How shall I know this? For I am an old man, and my wife is well advanced in years." [19] And the angel answered and said to him, "I am Gabriel, who stands in the presence of God, and was sent to speak to you and bring you these glad tidings. [20] "But behold, you will be mute and not able to speak until the day these things take place, because you did not believe my words which will be fulfilled in their own time." [21] And the people waited for Zacharias, and marveled that he lingered so long in the temple. [22] But when he came out, he could not speak to them; and they perceived that he had seen a vision in the temple, for he beckoned to them and remained speechless. [23] So it was, as soon as the days of his service were completed, that he departed to his own house. [24] Now after those days his wife Elizabeth conceived; and she hid herself five months, saying, [25] "Thus the Lord has dealt with me, in the days when He looked on me, to take away my reproach among people."

Devotion

The birth of Jesus Christ is not the only miraculous birth involved in the Christmas story. The miraculous birth of John the Baptist is a beautiful picture of the sovereign plan of God and the new life that accompanied the coming of the Savior to earth. Like so many in history before, Zechariah and his wife Elizabeth had spent their lives deprived of children. They surely had prayed and fasted, sacrificed, and sought medical treatments available to them. They could not have known that like Abraham and Sarah before them, their pain and struggle were to be used in the plan of God to magnify the coming Savior.

We encounter Zechariah first ministering in the temple. He had been given the special honor of being the priest who would enter the holy place in the temple to burn the incense that could only be made for use in the temple. This incense symbolizes the prayers of the saints in the book of Revelation. He would be one of but a relative few people in history who would be privileged to enter into that holy building and burn incense on that altar. Did he ask himself why God had never heard his fervent prayers over the years? We do not know. Though the plan of God had denied him a child thus far in his life we see that he faithfully served God. He was able to glorify

God in spite of the unfulfilled longing of his heart. According to Jewish tradition, childlessness was a legitimate reason for divorce. Yet, Zechariah never sent Elizabeth away. They waited upon the Lord.

When the angel Gabriel approached Zechariah he was justifiably amazed and frightened. After being reassured by the angelic messenger Zechariah is told that the Lord has heard his prayer - Elizabeth would bear a child. Imagine what effect those words would have on an old man whose wife was well past the age when women would become pregnant? Not only would they have a child, but that child would have a special place in God's plan. Zechariah's son would be the prophesied forerunner of the Messiah. Finding it difficult to understand (much less believe), Zechariah asks for a sign and is made mute until the birth of John. It is an interesting application to note that unbelief causes Zechariah to lose the ability to tell the world about the miracle. Be that as it may, the miraculous muteness would certify the truth and reality of the vision and promise that Zechariah received.

We are left to wonder what thoughts Zechariah considered until his prayer of praise. To rejoice in the answering of a lifelong prayer, to wonder in awe at the miraculous vision of the angel Gabriel. The Messiah was coming and his son would be the Holy Herald and the greatest of all the prophets.

DECEMBER 20TH

Luke 1:26-38

[26] Now in the sixth month the angel Gabriel was sent by God to a city of Galilee named Nazareth, [27] to a virgin betrothed to a man whose name was Joseph, of the house of David. The virgin's name was Mary. [28] And having come in, the angel said to her, "Rejoice, highly favored one, the Lord is with you; blessed are you among women!" [29] But when she saw him, she was troubled at his saying, and considered what manner of greeting this was. [30] Then the angel said to her, "Do not be afraid, Mary, for you have found favor with God. [31] "And behold, you will conceive in your womb and bring forth a Son, and shall call His name JESUS. [32] "He will be great, and will be called the Son of the Highest; and the Lord God will give Him the throne of His father David. [33] "And He will reign over the house of Jacob forever, and of His kingdom there will be no end." [34] Then Mary said to the angel, "How can this be, since I do not know a man?" [35] And the angel answered and said to her,

"The Holy Spirit will come upon you, and the power of the Highest will overshadow you; therefore, also, that Holy One who is to be born will be called the Son of God. [36] "Now indeed, Elizabeth your relative has also conceived a son in her old age; and this is now the sixth month for her who was called barren. [37] "For with God nothing will be impossible." [38] Then Mary said, "Behold the maidservant of the Lord! Let it be to me according to your word." And the angel departed from her.

Devotion

For Mary it may have been just another day. The day the angel Gabriel entered her company and told her something that would change her life forever. Luke's note is interesting. Mary is not surprised only by the angelic appearance, but by the greeting that He used. After all, what greeting should an angel use? This greeting appeared before in the Bible. The statement that "the Lord is with you" is given in the Bible in the context of military conflict. (Genesis 26:28; Numbers 14:9; Judges 6:12; 1 Samuel 16:18; 2 Chronicles 20:17). Why would an angel appear to her and give her a war-time greeting? It would perplex anyone.

Mary is told that she has found favor with God. The word "favor" is a grace-concept. It has to do with unmerited favor based upon the goodness of God. No one could deserve or earn this gift. The gift of being the vessel through whom God would bring the promised Messiah - the Savior! That is a great deal for any girl of around 14 to receive. More information is given about this Messiah she will bear into this world.

He would be great and called "Son of the Most High." By itself this is a clear statement of the deity of the Messiah. While the deity of the Messiah was clear from scripture the Jewish people had not yet come to understand. That very fact that was now laid bare before this young jewish girl.

The reality and anticipation of the coming Kingdom is the next topic. This Child would sit on the throne of His father David. The Messiah was a literal descendant of David according to His earthly lineage and he would sit on the throne of

David. David's throne was literal, physical, earthly, and actual. Solomon sat on that throne as did many of the other descendants of David. There is only one way that Mary could understand this precious promise - Jesus would be the promised one who would rule and reign over the literal, physical, actual nation of Israel. The duration of her Son's reign was also remarkable - it would be unending. Once Jesus takes that seat His reign will not end but will continue through the Millennial Kingdom and into the New Heavens and the New Earth for all eternity. This was a unique child indeed.

Mary's mind is drawn to the obvious difficulty. She was a virgin and thus could not logically be able to bear a child. Gabriel deals differently with Mary's question than with Zechariah's question. One wonders if the attitude of faith was different. Zechariah asked for a sign, where Mary asked for clarification. Whatever the case, Mary is given an explanation. That explanation was amazing. This conception would be miraculous - a work of the Holy Spirit of God.

Of course, that explanation would do little to appease her family, her fiance, and her friends. Would they ever believe that this Child was from God? When anyone else became pregnant outside of wedlock the shame was public and would last throughout a woman's life as well as the Child's life. Yet, Mary seemingly dismisses these practical concerns and responds in faith. Mary is pointed to one person at least who will believe and understand. Elizabeth was also experiencing a miraculous pregnancy of her own. The Lord provided someone for her to share the joy of this miracle. So Mary could go and visit her aunt, which she did.

First she responds with a most noble and faithful statement: "Behold the maidservant of the Lord! Let it be to me according to your word." Setting aside all personal concerns or questions Mary boldly presented herself to the Lord's use and glory. In a most unique way, Mary was the first person to have an experience of what Paul wrote in Colossians 1:27: "Christ in you, the hope of glory." And while the situation is markedly different between Mary and every believer today there is an important point of similarity: the world still does not understand. The one in whom Christ dwells may yet experience persecution and shame at the hands of the world. Jesus Christ is still the only hope for life, forgiveness, and salvation.

The Gift of Christmas

DECEMBER 21ST

Luke 1:39-56

[39] Now Mary arose in those days and went into the hill country with haste, to a city of Judah, [40] and entered the house of Zacharias and greeted Elizabeth. [41] And it happened, when Elizabeth heard the greeting of Mary, that the babe leaped in her womb; and Elizabeth was filled with the Holy Spirit. [42] Then she spoke out with a loud voice and said,

"Blessed are you among women, and blessed is the fruit of your womb! [43] "But why is this granted to me, that the mother of my Lord should come to me? [44] "For indeed, as soon as the voice of your greeting sounded in my ears, the babe leaped in my womb for joy. [45] "Blessed is she who believed, for there will be a fulfillment of those things which were told her from the Lord."

[46] And Mary said:
"My soul magnifies the Lord,

⁴⁷ And my spirit has rejoiced in God my Savior.
⁴⁸ For He has regarded the lowly state of His maidservant;
For behold, henceforth all generations will call me blessed.
⁴⁹ For He who is mighty has done great things for me,
And holy is His name.
⁵⁰ And His mercy is on those who fear Him
From generation to generation.
⁵¹ He has shown strength with His arm;
He has scattered the proud in the imagination of their hearts.
⁵² He has put down the mighty from their thrones,
And exalted the lowly.
⁵³ He has filled the hungry with good things,
And the rich He has sent away empty.
⁵⁴ He has helped His servant Israel,
In remembrance of His mercy,
⁵⁵ As He spoke to our fathers,
To Abraham and to his seed forever."

⁵⁶ And Mary remained with her about three months, and returned to her house.

Devotion

Imagine the journey of Mary to be with Elizabeth. If she chose not to share the story of Gabriel's appearance to her she may yet have been able to conceal her pregnancy. We can only wonder if she was always assured or if she wondered if what she had been told was true. Surely it could have been a dream, or a hallucination...yet the definite reality of the Life that she felt growing within her would cause her to consider the whole encounter over and over again. Encountering Elizabeth had to be a moment of deepest joy and confirmation. She was met with shame or questioning but with the recognition of God's work within Mary. The two women celebrated the goodness of God together.

Elizabeth sees the whole picture because the unborn child in her womb leapt for joy to be close to the Messiah. As has been well pointed out by many others: the first person (apart from Mary) on earth to recognize the Messiah was an unborn child! Elizabeth is then filled with the Holy Spirit and enters into making a declaration of praise by way of direct revelation. Mary was blessed indeed to have been given this special mission by God. Elizabeth was blessed and honored that the earthly mother of the Messiah would come and visit her! Mary's special blessing in the circumstance is related to her belief in the promise and plan that the Lord had revealed to her.

Mary responds with one of the greatest songs of praise ever written. Today we call this song the Magnificat. Mary sees her true purpose - and the purpose of all humanity: to magnify the glory of the Lord. That Child that God had given her to bear into this world would be the center of the fulfillment of God's every promise. He would be the living fulfillment of God's character and faithfulness and whatever the people of her day may think or say, the generations that would follow would know and call her blessed indeed. To feel the Son of God gently kicking within her womb. To see his little infant hand wrapped around her fingers. To know the Son of God in a way that no other human in all of history ever had or ever would. How good the Lord is to His servants who respond to His promises and provision in simple belief.

DECEMBER 22ND

Matthew 1:18-25

[18] Now the birth of Jesus Christ was as follows: After His mother Mary was betrothed to Joseph, before they came together, she was found with child of the Holy Spirit. [19] Then Joseph her husband, being a just man, and not wanting to make her a public example, was minded to put her away secretly. [20] But while he thought about these things, behold, an angel of the Lord appeared to him in a dream, saying, "Joseph, son of David, do not be afraid to take to you Mary your wife, for that which is conceived in her is of the Holy Spirit. [21] "And she will bring forth a Son, and you shall call His name JESUS, for He will save His people from their sins."

[22] So all this was done that it might be fulfilled which was spoken by the Lord through the prophet, saying: [23] "Behold, the virgin shall be with child, and bear a Son, and they shall call His name Immanuel," which is translated, "God with us."

[24] Then Joseph, being aroused from sleep, did as the angel of the Lord commanded him and took to him his wife, [25] and did not know her till she had brought forth her firstborn Son. And he called His name JESUS.

Devotion

Matthew begins the account of the Nativity with Jesus' father by adoption: Joseph. Luke details the story as it relates to Mary. Having heard that she was going to carry the Messiah she went to spend three months with her relative Elizabeth. It would not be uncommon, as in any age, for a younger woman to go and help a family member in a special situation. There would be little reason to talk around the village when she left. When she returned three months later, probably well into her second trimester of pregnancy, there was no hiding Mary's situation. Of course, being pregnant out of wedlock was shocking and would have massive repercussions, but the fact that Mary was engaged to Joseph made the situation even more complicated.

In first-century Israel, marriage was a very important process with several steps. If a man wished to propose to a woman, he would go with his father and speak to her father. If the parents agreed that the marriage was good, then the bride-to-be was invited into the room and the groom would present her with a cup of wine. Should she wish to marry him then she would take the cup of wine. Should she not wish to marry him then she would refuse the cup of wine. Mary had already agreed to this engagement with Joseph. The couple was then regarded as married but they were not permitted to have sexual relations with one another until their wedding. If the couple should be sexually involved with one another it would be considered sinful. Were they to be involved with anyone else it would be treated as adultery. If they were to wish to end the engagement they would need to procure a divorce.

There were two religious courts in Israel to which a person would report to obtain a divorce. Each court was named after an important Jewish Rabbi who headed a particular school of thought. These two rabbis were Rabbi Hillel and Rabbi Shammai. These two courts had different views on divorce. The Court of Shammai was strict and would only allow divorce under a few circumstances, one of which was sexual immorality. In order to get a divorce in the court of Shammai there had to be public recognition of who sinned and what they did.

The other court was the court of Hillel and this court allowed a person to get a divorce for any reason, no matter how petty. In this court, a man could divorce his wife for burning his dinner (really!). The court of Hillel had a sort of "no-fault" divorce that allowed people to quietly divorce one another.

The evidence (Mary's pregnancy) was clear that Joseph could pursue a legal divorce in either court. The fact that Mary's apparent infidelity had publicly shamed him would cause a vengeful person to want to come before the court of Shammai. Joseph shows his merciful character in wanting to "divorce her quietly" - he wanted to go privately to the court of Hillel and procure a divorce so that Mary would not experience any more public difficulty or shame than was necessary. Setting aside his own feelings he wanted what would be best for Mary in that situation as she had apparently rejected him.

It is at this point that an angel appears to Joseph in a dream. The angel addresses Joseph as a son of David. The angel is recognizing that Joseph is indeed the correct Davidic heir. We may wonder why Joseph lived so humbly if he truly was the heir of David. As the Bible account shows, Herod had wrongfully claimed that title. Herod the Great was so jealous of his crown that he even killed his own children, and later killed all of the children in Bethlehem to eliminate a would-be contender for the throne. It makes sense that Joseph was keeping that quiet, given the situation. However, there are no secrets from God. He had followed and protected this special line so that when the time came for the Messiah to arrive - the lineage would be perfect.

The angel then explains the situation. Mary's pregnancy was supernatural. This fulfilled the virgin birth prophecy in the book of Isaiah. Furthermore, Joseph and Mary would not be free to name this Child. God Himself decreed the name of this Child for several reasons. First, as created beings, they did not have the authority to name the Son of God. Second, the name "Jesus" has meaning. Jesus truly is the salvation provided by God. Finally, the name translated as "Jesus" is, in Hebrew, "Yeshua" or "Joshua." The name "Joshua" has significance in the Old Testament and Joshua was the man chosen by God to lead Israel into the promised land. So, Jesus is the One who will lead the world into the future Messianic Kingdom.
Joseph chose to do what the Lord commanded because the hope of the messianic promise is worth whatever shame or humiliation may come forth. Joseph is an example of faithfulness to the Lord and willingness to obey Him.

The Gift of Christmas

DECEMBER 23RD

Luke 2:1-7

[1] And it came to pass in those days that a decree went out from Caesar Augustus that all the world should be registered. [2] This census first took place while Quirinius was governing Syria. [3] So all went to be registered, everyone to his own city. [4] Joseph also went up from Galilee, out of the city of Nazareth, into Judea, to the city of David, which is called Bethlehem, because he was of the house and lineage of David, [5] to be registered with Mary, his betrothed wife, who was with child. [6] So it was, that while they were there, the days were completed for her to be delivered. [7] And she brought forth her firstborn Son, and wrapped Him in swaddling cloths, and laid Him in a manger, because there was no room for them in the inn.

Devotion

Prophecy was in trouble. Mary had the right genealogy and had been told how the miraculous prophecy that the Messiah would be born of a virgin would be fulfilled. There was a serious risk that Joseph would choose to ignore God's plan and choose to divorce Mary "quietly." The Lord stepped in with a dream to explain to Joseph what was going on and what needed to be done by Joseph. Joseph responded in faith and obedience and it became clear for the first time in history how the Messiah could come from the ruling line of David, yet not be affected by the curse on the line of Jechoniah. As Jesus would be the legal adopted son of Joseph He would be the rightful heir to David's throne and to all of the messianic promises. But there was still a problem: the geography.

As we know, Jesus was born in Bethlehem...but Joseph and Mary lived in Nazareth. What possible reason would they possibly have to relocate at such a sensitive time in life. Anyone who has had a child knows the difficulties and stresses of the final months of pregnancy, the dangers of birth, and the difficulties of raising an infant. It is most natural that Mary would want to be around her family in this important time. Her family would surely want the same thing! Yet, God had put forth in Micah 5:3 that the Messiah would be born in the city of David - Bethlehem Ephrathah.

We do not know what would have caused the family of Joseph - the rightful heir of the Davidic throne - to move to Nazareth. It could well be that in light of all of the political drama and the unpredictable violence of Herod the Great that they chose to get of a dangerous place some generations ago. Whatever the case, if scripture were to be fulfilled, something would have to happen. God displayed His sovereignty over even the greatest government that had ever been seen on the earth: Rome.

Rome was a new kind of empire. The kind that would largely leave you alone if you paid your taxes and stayed in line. Taxation involved some problems. Keeping track of the many people of the Roman empire - whether they were alive or dead - meant a lot of work for quite a few people. A census was a way to see how many people were in the Roman Empire and what their tax burden should be. Ordering those people became an issue. If you count households, you have an issue because a family could be spread over a great distance. The brilliant idea to get everybody to return to their ancestral homeland was the solution. Everyone just had to get to their family's hometown to be counted.

For Joseph that meant going on a journey. A journey from Nazareth to Bethlehem would be 70 miles as the crow flies. In all practicality that meant a 4-day journey for most. The popular myth that Mary and Joseph had a donkey is possible, but by no means certain. It is quite likely that a very pregnant Mary had a 5-day walk in order to find themselves in Bethlehem. Scripture tells us that they arrived just in time. It is an amazing feature of the Christmas story -

God moved the greatest empire the world had ever seen in order to fulfill prophecy so that the Messiah would be born in exactly the right place.

DECEMBER 24ᵀᴴ

Luke 2:8-20

[8] Now there were in the same country shepherds living out in the fields, keeping watch over their flock by night. [9] And behold, an angel of the Lord stood before them, and the glory of the Lord shone around them, and they were greatly afraid.

[10] Then the angel said to them, "Do not be afraid, for behold, I bring you good tidings of great joy which will be to all people. [11] "For there is born to you this day in the city of David a Savior, who is Christ the Lord. [12] "And this will be the sign to you: You will find a Babe wrapped in swaddling cloths, lying in a manger."

[13] And suddenly there was with the angel a multitude of the heavenly host praising God and saying: [14] "Glory to God in the highest, And on earth peace, goodwill toward men!"

[15] So it was, when the angels had gone away from

them into heaven, that the shepherds said to one another, "Let us now go to Bethlehem and see this thing that has come to pass, which the Lord has made known to us."

[16] And they came with haste and found Mary and Joseph, and the Babe lying in a manger. [17] Now when they had seen Him, they made widely known the saying which was told them concerning this Child. [18] And all those who heard it marveled at those things which were told them by the shepherds. [19] But Mary kept all these things and pondered them in her heart. [20] Then the shepherds returned, glorifying and praising God for all the things that they had heard and seen, as it was told them.

Devotion

You can tell how important a party is simply by checking the guest list. A party filled with celebrities and world leaders is sure to generate some attention. By contrast the Christmas party of the local garage is far less likely to draw a crowd. When Jesus Christ came into the world the best and brightest on the world scene were not invited. That doesn't mean the guest list wasn't distinguished. Quite to the contrary, the great Gift of Heaven was witnessed by exactly the right people.

As occupations go, shepherds were not at the top of the social ladder. Spending nearly every moment with the sheep meant that they would often be dirty and smelly by the city-dweller's assessment. More importantly than that, shepherding was a 24-hour a day job. That meant that it would be difficult to get into town for social gatherings or to fulfill religious obligations. Shepherds were also in regular contact with dead animal corpses, which would render them ceremonially unclean. In modern terms, nobody would put shepherds on their list of prestigious career aspirations.

Nevertheless, the shepherds in this account were very special indeed. Many have pointed out the fact that the Lord's announcement to these shepherds highlights the reality that Christ Jesus came for ALL. Not just the wealthy, powerful, or impressive - but for the humble and lowly. This is true. Others have pointed out that all of the city folk were locked away inside. They were busy with all their many important obligations at home. The shepherds were available. The simplicity of their lives watching the sheep made them the perfect candidates to see the

angelic band that would announce the Messiah's
birth. There is something else that is interesting
about the shepherds of this region.

The shepherds of this region would be raising
the lambs that would be offered at the Passover. This
was an important job as the Old Testament had
certain requirements for those lambs that would be
offered on this important day in Israel's religious
calendar. The Passover is the annual celebration of
the time that God released Israel from slavery in
Egypt. God used Moses and Aaron to tell the
Pharaoh to free Israel. Upon Pharaoh's refusal the
Lord used plagues to show Pharaoh that He was
serious, and that He had the power to make this
demand. The Jews were God's people, not Pharaoh's
people. The final plague was the plague of the
firstborn. The firstborn of every household in Egypt
would die. The only escape from this plague was for
a lamb to be killed, and the blood had to be painted
upon the doorposts of the home. That lamb died in
order to save those believers inside.

These shepherds would be looking after the
lines of these sheep since a sheep and its mother
could not be sacrificed on the same day. They would
be well versed in looking and knowing which lambs
were perfect - and which were blemished. These
shepherds were always looking for the lamb that
would be a good sacrifice. On this night they would
see The Lamb that would be qualified to make the
sacrifice that would bring salvation to all who would
believe. Oh, and did I mention that there were angels
as well?

God sent an angelic messenger to notify
Zechariah of the coming miraculous birth of John the

Baptist. An angel was sent to let Mary know that she was the blessed woman who would bear the Messiah through most miraculous means. An angel appeared to Joseph in a dream to explain everything and keep the course of prophecy intact. And then *a multitude* of angels were deployed to make sure that the shepherds would be there. They revealed to this unkempt group of laborers that the Messiah had been born this day…and was to be found in a feeding trough for animals.

The shepherds did something that shepherds never did. They left the flock. They left their post because they *had* to see this promised Savior. They went through the town looking, hunting, and searching for this babe lying in a manger. They found Him. Have you?

The Gift of Christmas

DECEMBER 25TH

John 1:1-18

¹ In the beginning was the Word, and the Word was with God, and the Word was God. ² He was in the beginning with God. ³ All things were made through Him, and without Him nothing was made that was made. ⁴ In Him was life, and the life was the light of men. ⁵ And the light shines in the darkness, and the darkness did not comprehend it.

⁶ There was a man sent from God, whose name was John. ⁷ This man came for a witness, to bear witness of the Light, that all through him might believe. ⁸ He was not that Light, but was sent to bear witness of that Light. ⁹ That was the true Light which gives light to every man coming into the world. ¹⁰ He was in the world, and the world was made through Him, and the world did not know Him. ¹¹ He came to His own, and His own did not receive Him. ¹² But as many as received Him, to them He gave the right to become children of God, to those who believe in His name: ¹³

who were born, not of blood, nor of the will of the flesh, nor of the will of man, but of God. [14] And the Word became flesh and dwelt among us, and we beheld His glory, the glory as of the only begotten of the Father, full of grace and truth.

[15] John bore witness of Him and cried out, saying, "This was He of whom I said, 'He who comes after me is preferred before me, for He was before me.' " [16] And of His fullness we have all received, and grace for grace. 17 For the law was given through Moses, but grace and truth came through Jesus Christ. [18] No one has seen God at any time. The only begotten Son, who is in the bosom of the Father, He has declared Him.

Devotion

Matthew and Luke provide complementary accounts of the Nativity. Each highlights different events and details surrounding the birth of the Holy Child. Tradition tell us that John outlived the rest of the apostolic band. Most of them had died martyrs' deaths years before John would pen these beautiful and theologically important words. John had nothing to add to the events surrounding the Messiah's birth. He had a great deal say on the topic regarding its significance.

At the beginning of all things - when God spoke the heavens and the earth into being - the Word (*logos* in Greek - in Hebrew *memra*). The full expression of God, the Son of God, already existed. He was with God. He was unique in person and had an individual identity. He *was* God. Co-equal and co-eternal with God the Father and God the Holy Spirit. The Second Member of the Trinity was one in essence with God the Father and everything that is true of God the Father is true of God the Son. This *Word* was the essential agent in Creation of the world. The whole world was made by Him and everything was designed to know and obey Him as the Creator.

On that first Christmas morning the *Word* became flesh. The Greek word translated "dwelt" alludes to the idea of dwelling in a tent. Before, God's special presence was in the Tabernacle. The meeting place between God and man in the Old Testament finally found its fulfillment when the Son of God *tabernacled* among us. Those who knew Him could say, with all honesty, that they beheld the glory of God. Moses asked to see the glory of the Lord

119

and could only stand to see that glory as he passed. Peter, James, and John went to the mount of Transfiguration and saw that glory. John, in retrospect, would make it clear: Anyone who sees Jesus sees the glory of God.

Jesus came to the earth so that those who believed in Him would have life through His Name. By faith in Jesus Christ any sinner is given the right to be called a child of God. On Christmas day we celebrate this One - Jesus Christ - the Glory of God revealed, the love of God made clear, and the salvation of God made available to every soul who trusts in Him.

The Gift of Christmas

The Gift of Christmas

The Gift of Christmas

The Gift of Christmas

ABOUT THE AUTHOR

Dr. Bradley W. Maston is the husband of April Maston and the father of four beautiful children. He has walked with Jesus for 20 years and served Him as a missionary, music pastor, youth minister and he is currently the Pastor of Fort Collins Bible Church (www.fortcollinsbiblechurch.com) in beautiful Fort Collins, Colorado. Bradley has a passion for the study and exposition of the Bible and his published works seek to make Jesus known.